The Making of a Man

The Power of Image and Reflection

Dr. Jamie T. Pleasant; Ph.D.

The Making of

a Man

The Power of Image and Reflection

Dr. Jamie T. Pleasant; Ph.D.

The Making of a Man: The Power of Image and Reflection

Copyright © 2015 by Dr. Jamie T. Pleasant; Ph.D.

Biblion Publishing LLC

All rights reserved. No portion of this book may be reproduced, stored in a retrieval system or transmitted in any form or by any means — electronic, mechanical, photocopy, recording or other without the prior written authorization of the author — except for a brief quotation in printed reviews.

Unless otherwise indicated, scripture quotations are from the Holy Bible, Modern English Version.

First Edition / First Printing

ISBN-978-1-940698-01-4

Table of Contents

Chapter 1	What is a Man?	15
Chapter 2	It Takes a Man to Make a Man	23
Chapter 3	A Man Knows How to Live	31
Chapter 4	A Man Knows His Place in Life	41
Chapter 5	A Man Loves His Work	49
Chapter 6	A Man Walks in Integrity	59
Chapter 7	A Man Possesses Wisdom	67
Chapter 8	Only God Can Make a Man	75

The Making of a Man!

Your age, height, weight, strength and accomplishments alone are not enough to classify you as a man! What is the makeup of a man? Are you sure that you have reached manhood? How do you know if you have or not? This book answers these questions. Get ready to experience what it really means to be a man. Do you want to fully enter manhood? Do you want to know for sure that you have been properly prepared to be a man? If so, this book is for you! *"The Making of a Man"* will take you on a journey to uncovering the man in you that God designed you to be. Each chapter presents straightforward principles and steps to becoming a man of God by his original design that began in the Garden of Eden with a man named Adam. You will reach new heights in your personal walk into manhood! You will learn how to become a man and make men as well.

Dedication

To my Daddy, Anthony T. Pleasant, who was a perfect example to me of a real man. To my wife Kimberly (oh, how I love you darling!), my two sons; Christian and Zion, and daughter, Nacara.

To the late, great Mr. Muldrow Burgess, who was a second father to me and influenced my life in so many ways. You are the most intelligent man I have ever known in my life. You made me who I have become academically and professionally. I always wanted to grow up to be like you. I hope I did! To my New Zion Christian Church Family, how I love you so much. I am the most blessed Pastor in the world because of you. You make it so easy! I speak blessings in all of your lives.

Humbly Yours in Christ,

Apostle Jamie T. Pleasant

Getting the most out of "The Making of a Man"

Congratulations on purchasing this book! Get ready to take your journey into manhood to a new level. This book includes eight chapters of inspiring and instructional teachings concerning manhood. You can use this book for personal growth or group study sessions. All of the scriptures are from the Modern English Version (MEV) Bible translation (unless otherwise noted). Each lesson, will take you on a journey into manhood based on Biblical principles that can be practically applied in your daily life. Sit back, relax, and become the man God designed you to be.

Chapter 1

What Is a Man?

Genesis 1:26 (MEV)

²⁶ Then God said, "Let us make man in <u>our image,</u> after <u>our likeness</u>, and let them have dominion over the fish of the sea, and over the birds of the air, and over the livestock, and over all the earth, and over every creeping thing that creeps on the earth."

Your age, weight, height and strength alone are not enough to classify you as a man. You are not qualified to be a man just because you have a job and make a certain amount of money. In fact, the type of car you drive or the clothes you wear do not make you a man. The number of children you have definitely does not qualify you to call yourself a man. If you define yourself as a man based on these attainments or characteristics, you mistakenly classify yourself.

Since the above-mentioned characteristics and accomplishments don't classify you as a man, then what is a man? Let's take a deeper look at what a man actually is. The Theological Wordbook of the Old Testament *(TWOT) #25*, describes the word *man,* as one that is created in the image of God. This means that a man is a true representation and reflection of His creator, Jehovah God. That means, every time others see a man, they will see God in that man! A man will reflect God's glory, presence and being.

> **A man will reflect God's glory, presence and being.**

According to the Bible, a man is not created *"by His image"*, but *"in His image"*. This means that everything God is, everything He represents and everything God is known to be, was placed in a

What is a Man?

man. A man was created out of all of the characteristics of who God is. Love, mercy, compassion and goodness are key characteristics that make-up and define who God is and are to be reflected in a man. Therefore, a man should represent God this way in everything that he does. In other words, we have been placed on this earth as God's representative of how life should be lived as an example to others. A man should talk like God! Think like God! Act like God! Sound like God! And most of all, perfectly reflect and represent God! When others encounter a man, they should be in awe and respect of his being. That means that a man's attitude and actions should demand attention in a positive regard. We should not be cursing, lying, cheating, stealing, etc. Those things don't make you a man. They do the exact opposite. They make you look like less of a man. In fact, cursing, bragging about how many women you have had relations with, lying, etc., only shows that you are trying to define your manhood because you haven't been defined by God yet.

> **In fact, cursing, bragging about how many women you have had relations with, lying, etc., only shows that you are trying to define your manhood because you haven't been defined by God yet.**

When a man has been defined by God, he becomes refined in the way he does everything. His actions are Godly, Holy and upright. He is refined in the sense that he has been made in the image of God, perfected by the grace of God, strengthened by the Spirit of God, and equipped to be successful through the knowledge of God. When someone encounters a man like you, there should be a presence about you that says that you are a special person with special attributes. When people encounter you, they should want to emulate you. A man changes the people around him. A

What is a Man?

man changes the atmosphere. He creates an environment of positive change and growth. A man demands people to take notice that he is uniquely endowed with special abilities given to him by God to do certain things that will enhance and enrich other's lives that he comes into contact with. Are you a man? Or, are you fooling yourself? Have you positively influenced anyone's life? Have you been in a stressful situation that you could have easily cursed or acted in haste with anger, but instead you showed wisdom and responded calmly? Has anyone ever told you that you display an attitude that is Christ-like? If you can't answer any of these questions positively, you aren't a man yet. Understand that a man is not perfect. However, he is striving to be the best representative and reflection of God that he can be. Therefore, sometimes a man may have a bad behavior day, but his good behavior days should outweigh his bad behavior days.

What is a Man?

> **A man may have a bad behavior day, but his good behavior days should outweigh his bad behavior days.**

Don't get mad or upset as you evaluate your development as a man in this book. Develop a mindset that you will become a positive reflection and true representative of God! This book will get you there.

What is a Man?

Reflection

What is a man?

_____
_____
_____

What does it mean to be created in the image of God?

_____
_____
_____

Write below a time that you have been a positive influence in someone's life.

_____
_____
_____

Explain how you acted with Christ-like character in a stressful situation in your life.

_____
_____
_____
_____

What is a Man?

Chapter 2

It Takes a Man to Make a Man

Genesis 1:27 (MEV)

So <u>God created man</u> in <u>His own image</u>; in the image of God He created him;

Notice that God created man. Notice also that it was *in the image* of God that man was created. What does that mean? It means that the image that a male child sees in his father will make him into whom he will be. A male child will become the exact representation of the image that he sees of his father. Isn't it interesting that if a male child comes from a family where his father physically and or verbally abuses his wife, that male child has a higher probability of growing up and abusing his wife as well. If a male child grows up in a home where the father is never there, he will become the same way in his home when he has a family. A male child will replicate the image of what he sees in his father.

> **A male child will replicate the image of what he sees in his father.**

The only way a male child will change any negative behavior he sees in his father, is to become exposed to an image from another Godly man. For some, that will happen with the contact he makes with a coach, Pastor, teacher or family member. Sadly, many young males will begin to identify with someone in their neighborhood or school that might not be a positive reflection of God and His glorious characteristics. The most assured way to change the behavior of a young male that has never seen a positive Godly image

It Takes a Man to Make a Man

of a man in his life, is for him to become saved and seek God to create a new image for him to see.

Notice that the scripture says, So God created man in His own image; <u>in the image of God, He created him.</u> This sheds insight for us to see that it is, *"in the image of God"* that *"He creates"*. This hints that the man Adam was created as he saw the image of His creator. Do you get that? That means that Adam was only created as he was exposed to the image of the Father. To understand this more, a man can only be made as he is in the presence of another man because that is where creative power exists.

> **A man can only be made as he is in the presence of another man because that is where creative power exists.**

Imagine what would happen if Holy men of God around the world got together, held a meeting, and let their Godly images begin to reflect on each other. Imagine the creative power and positive changes that would take place! Imagine the dreams, visions, purposes and blessings that would manifest in that place! Imagine how families would be restored! Imagine how destinies would be set in place! Do you see what is taking place as you read this? You are imagining! You are imagining being in a place with other men and you can see great things happening can't you? If you are, you are giving off creative power that would manifest if there were another male around to see it and appreciate it. Adam was just not lying around during his creation. No! He was observing the image of all he saw in God and it gave him power to become a living being. How do we know this? Because, scripture says, *he was in his image*, not just being created *by his image*. Image is everything! God's image is more than everything. It is the only thing! God's image is waiting on you. Are you walking in it? Are you living up to it? Are you replicating His image given to you on someone else? Do you have a son that is the splitting image of you? Are you the splitting image of your father? You should be. You and I should be the splitting image of our Father Jehovah. We should talk, walk, speak, act and live just like Him.

It Takes a Man to Make a Man

Reflection

What does, *"it takes a man to make a man"* mean?

_____

_____

_____

Can you name a man that influenced your life and along with God, made you who you are today?

_____

_____

_____

How did this man influence your life?

_____

_____

_____

It Takes a Man to Make a Man

Name some people, including your children that you want to positively influence the lives of.

_____

_____

_____

What will you do to impact the lives of each person you named above?

_____

_____

_____

_____

_____

_____

_____

_____

_____

_____

Chapter 3

A Man Knows How to Live

Genesis 2:7 (MEV)

⁷ Then the LORD God formed man from the dust of the ground and <u>breathed into his nostrils</u> the breath of life, and <u>man became a living being</u>.

We see now how God makes man a living being. God breathes into the man and he then becomes a living being. It is the contact with God through the breath of His Spirit that makes man a living being. When a male comes into contact with God, he will become a living being.

> **When a male comes into contact with God, he will become a living being.**

What does it mean that when a male comes into contact with God, he will become a living being? Let's look at it. When a male can breathe, eat, think and move, he is alive. However, that doesn't mean that he is living. Being alive means a person is not dead and has a heartbeat on earth. Therefore, having a heartbeat means you are alive. For example, many people have a heartbeat but don't know that their heart is beating. Did you get that? There are many people that are unconscious of being in this world or even who they are as they are in a coma or on life support. They are not dead because their heart is still beating. However, they can't move on their own, eat on their own or even think. Therefore, they are alive but not living.

When a newborn baby boy enters the world, he is alive but he is not living because he is not conscious he is alive. He can't eat on his own, make a living for himself or anything like that. He doesn't know who his father or mother is. Anyone could take care of him and he would be just fine. When someone is living, they are aware of their surroundings and enjoy life. They are conscious of whom they are and all that is around them that is at their disposal ordained by God. That is the difference in living, not just being alive. A living being is conscious of his creator. He is aware of all creation! A living being is conscious of the creator whom makes all things, created things made for him and things he has been created to create! That's powerful knowledge to comprehend isn't it?

> **A living being is conscious of the creator whom makes all things, created things made for him and things he has been created to create!**

In other words, a man that is a living being will see his dreams take life! His purpose will take life! His destiny will take life. He will not only think about them, he will experience them. Most importantly, he will know that everything he has obtained and accomplished comes from his creator and would not have happened if it weren't for his creator whom is God Jehovah. He will become a new creation and walk in the promises and blessings of God that was intended uniquely for him. That is why opposing forces of God will do any and everything to stop men from being in unity and in the presence of each other. Opposing forces never want you to become conscious of your creator as He is making you. Being conscious is simply being aware and participatory of what is taking place in your life. God the Father wants you to watch Him as He makes you into a man of God! He wants you to watch Him as He makes you into a man of integrity! He wants you to watch Him make a way out of no way in your life! He wants you to watch! Therefore, we need to "be" as well as "do". That's right! In fact, we must become *"beings"* before we can become *"doers"*. There is a time to "be" and a time to "do". In fact, we have to "be" before we can "do". When we "be", God is filling us with His Spirit to have the ability to perform and function. After we are filled in our "being" state, we are then able to "do" or perform. We are then free to perform and accomplish things with ease and joy. That is living. Living is not working tirelessly until you can't stand up or become sick. That is not living, that is perishing. Living is putting in optimal effort for maximum results.

> **Living is putting in optimal effort for maximum results.**

Living is enjoying things and people in life. That can't be accomplished outside of God's grace and Spirit working within us.

So, let us look at this some more. Notice it is not God breathing into Adam's nostrils that makes him a living being. It is God breathing *the breath of life* into Adam that makes him a living being. In other words, it is the *breath of life*, which gave him the ability to become conscious of who he was and who his creator was whom entered his body. He then became a living being, aware of his surroundings, himself and a loving Father. Notice, Adam was not created a male child or baby. He was created a man. Manhood has nothing to do with being born and growing up, but everything to do with being created by God.

A Man Knows How to Live

> **Manhood has nothing to do with being born and growing up, but everything to do with being created by God.**

A male becomes a man when the breath of life is breathed into him. It takes a saved, anointed and Holy man of God to breathe life into a male and then instantly he will give his life to Christ and become a living being. It is important to note that it takes a man who is saved to breathe life into another male that will cause him to become a living being. Have you ever been around someone that said something to you or gave you advice and your entire perspective changed and you became enlightened and full of energy and enthusiasm? If so, that is because that person breathed the breath of life into you. Every day we are given the opportunity to breathe the breath of life in young males and help them become living beings. When we speak positive things in their lives, they will

A Man Knows How to Live

become living beings! When we share a word of wisdom with them, they become living beings! When we encourage them, they become living beings! A man knows how to live. He lives by giving life to young males!

> **A man knows how to live. He lives by giving life to young males!**

He gives life by sharing the Word of God with young males. He gives life by being a positive role model in his home and in his community. He gives life when he shares his time with a young male and mentors him. A man knows how to live. Christ was such a man. He gave his life that we would live. He was a perfect example of a man of God. We can act just like He did. Are you ready to begin your journey into manhood?

Reflection

Do you know how to live? If yes or no explain.

_____
_____
_____
_____

How can you breathe the breath of life into someone else?

_____
_____
_____
_____

How will you know when you have been created into a man?

_____
_____
_____
_____

Chapter 4

A Man Knows His Place in Life

Genesis 2:8 (MEV)
⁸ The LORD **God planted a <u>garden</u> in the <u>east</u>, in <u>Eden</u>, and there He placed the man whom He had formed.**

A man knows his place in life. He knows what he is supposed to be doing. He knows that God has prepared a place for him to be successful. It is important for every man to operate in the career that God has prepared for him before he was born. Notice that God planted the garden in the east of Eden first. The Garden of Eden was created before Adam was. Once God created the place for

A Man Knows His Place in Life

Adam to be successful, he placed him there. A man should always seek God and ask Him where it is that a prepared place has been made for him. We don't need to blindly choose our careers and where we should live etc. A man is always in such a great relationship with his Heavenly Father that he lets Him place him where he is supposed to be. Men don't move before knowing exactly where God has placed them.

> **Men don't move before knowing exactly where God has placed them.**

When God places a man, no one can move him from there. When God places a man, challenges, struggles, setbacks and disappointments will only make him stronger and complete in the bigger plan God has for his life. We should not move to a new job because of a pay increase or better position without making sure that God placed us in that position. Adam was placed in a prepared place where he would prosper and have authoritative control. When God places a man, he knows that God will protect, provide and establish him.

> **When God places a man, he knows that God will protect, provide and establish him.**

Notice that Adam was not placed in the Garden of Eden just anywhere. He was placed in the east of the garden in Eden. That means that Adam was given a particular area where he was to have rulership, authority and experience prosperity. His place of blessings was in the east of the Garden of Eden. This helps us to understand that as a man we have the pay attention to the details of our placement when God assigns a place for us. Therefore, we must think about any job offer that is presented to us. The job offer may

A Man Knows His Place in Life

be what we want, but is it where God placed us? Is it in the right city? Is it in the right department? Is it with the right company? Only a man of God in relationship with Him can properly discern these things. Let's look at Eden, where the man was placed. The Hebrew word, Eden *(ay'-den)*, from Strong's Greek & Hebrew Dictionary number 5730, means a place of delight and pleasure. Amazingly, Adam would find his delight and pleasure in the east portion of a place called, Eden. This was his home, his place to work and relax that God prepared and placed him to enjoy his life. A man will always find delight and pleasure in his home, work and life when he finds his place in life.

> **A man will always find delight and pleasure in his home, work and life when he finds his place in life.**

A Man Knows His Place in Life

He will find delight and pleasure there because he is in his sphere of blessings. Too many people have no delight or pleasure at home, work or any place else, because they are not in their place of blessing. Do you hate where you work? Do you find displeasure in your job? Are you always frustrated when you get home because of bad experiences you have on your job daily? If you answered yes to any of these questions, you are in the wrong place. We can only become a man when we are in the right place where God has ordained us to be.

> **We can only become a man when we are in the right place where God has ordained us to be.**

A Man Knows His Place in Life

Reflection

How will you know when you have found your place in life?

_____
_____
_____
_____

Have you found your place in life? Alternatively, are you still looking?

_____
_____
_____
_____

A Man Knows His Place in Life

What should your work environment be like?

_____

_____

_____

_____

What should your home life be like?

_____

_____

_____

_____

A Man Knows His Place in Life

Chapter 5

A Man Loves His Work

Genesis 2:15 (MEV)

¹⁵ The LORD God <u>took the man</u> and <u>put him</u> in the garden of Eden to <u>till it</u> and to <u>keep it</u>.

If you were to ask most people what is the one thing they would change in their life if they could, they would quickly tell you they wouldn't want to have to work every day. Most people want to be able to enjoy life and all of the things in it without having to work every day. Most people feel this way because they aren't working, they are enslaved! Being enslaved means, that someone is forced into something they don't want to do. They do it because they have to. Did you understand that? There is a difference between working and being enslaved.

> **There is a difference between working and being enslaved.**

Remember that God placed Adam in the east part of Eden which means, delight and pleasure. Now we see him giving Adam an assignment to *till* and *keep* the garden. How can Adam find delight and pleasure in tilling and keeping a garden? We know the garden wasn't cultivated, which means it wasn't developed or well manicured because it had never rained etc. in the garden at this time. We can see this in Genesis 2:5, where it says, [5] no shrub of the field was yet on the earth, and _no plant of the field had yet sprouted,_ for the LORD God had not caused it to rain on the earth, and

A Man Loves His Work

<u>there was no man to cultivate</u> the ground. So then, why would God place Adam in an uncultivated area to find pleasure and delight by tilling and keeping that place? Well, it is simple. God wanted Adam to assist Him in the completeness of His creation of earth. Remember that we learned earlier that a man creates with the creator. In other words, God designed man to assist him in the creative process of His divine design of the earth. Furthermore, God wanted Adam to till the area, not be enslaved by the area. That means God wanted Adam to dress, cultivate and beautify the place he would live in. Let's look at it another way. If you buy a home, would you want it predesigned with all the furniture, rooms and layout already in place? In other words, would you be happy with a house that had no electricity because the designer that you are buying the house from thinks that this is not important for you to have? How about if the designer of the house you

A Man Loves His Work

are buying doesn't believe in indoor toilets? What if he believes they are a waste of water resources, so he doesn't put any toilets in your predesigned house either? Wouldn't you feel uncomfortable, even to think about living in that house? On the other hand, would you rather buy a home that you help design, layout and choose your own furniture etc.? I know I would rather have a choice in as much of the new move into the house as possible. I would like to decorate, arrange and make the house my home. By adding my personal touches in the plans, furniture selections, etc., it would become and feel like it was mine.

That is exactly what God was doing with Adam in the Garden of Eden. He wanted Adam to make his home feel like it was his. He wanted Adam to till the garden. To till means to dress, cultivate and beautify. In other words, God wanted Adam to make it his own! When you dress,

A Man Loves His Work

cultivate or beautify something, you are not slaving! You are not miserable! You are full of joy because you are expressing and putting your personal touch on something. You are creating something that is an outward expression of you! You are simply making it yours to your liking, pleasure and comfort. That is what God wanted Adam to do. He wanted Adam to participate in the creative process.

As a man, we are created by God to work. We are created to make things beautiful, pleasing and manageable. When a man is busy creating, beautifying, dressing and making things better for himself, family and others in this life; he can take pleasure and delight in that. A man knows that if his work doesn't provide joy, delight and pleasure for him, he is in the wrong place. A man should get excited when it's time to go to work and feel a little empty when it's time to stop working.

A Man Loves His Work

> **A man should get excited when it's time to go to work and feel a little empty when it's time to stop working.**

As much as he should feel a little emptiness at the end of his workday, he should immediately find a newfound joy and excitement because he is on his way home to be with his family where there is even more delight and pleasure. If you are not happy when you go to work, you are not placed correctly. Seek God and ask Him to direct you to your place of work where delight and pleasure awaits you!

Notice also that Adam is to keep the Garden of Eden. The Hebrew word for *"keep"* means to *guard and protect*. Why would God tell the man he is to guard and protect the garden? Why is that so important? God knows that someone else is watching Adam and jealous of what has been given to him. Not only is that someone else jealous, he is envious of the relationship that Adam and God have. That someone else will do whatever he can to take what has been given to Adam. We know satan is that someone else. God wants to bless Adam and give him a great place to live. God knows satan will be coming soon to try to take Adam out of the joy and blessings of God. He knows he will try to corrupt this area of the Garden of Eden that Adam has been placed in. Therefore, God first requires Adam to put his personal touch in his place so that he won't let anyone come and take what is his. He wants Adam to feel that all that he has put into it would be too much to lose to satan. God wanted Adam to love his area. What a man works for, he loves. That what he loves, he keeps and cares for.

> **What a man works for he loves. That what he loves, he keeps and cares for.**

A Man Loves His Work

A man will protect, fight and care for everything that he loves. He loves what he works for. He works for what he loves to care for. Interestingly, many people treat their family members wrong and are very mean to them. These people are not happy with where they have been placed in life to work. As a result, of being miserable at their place of work, they are miserable with all that are closest to them. Unfortunately, those closest to them are their family members whom they are supposed to love. God designed man to be placed in an environment where he experiences delight and pleasure while working. God also wants a man to protect, provide and nurture those he has been placed to love in the area assigned for him to prosper and live.

Reflection

Do you love your work? Explain why or why not?

_____
_____
_____
_____

What is the difference between work and enslavement?

_____
_____
_____
_____

If you had $10 million dollars cash, what would you do to stay busy and productive to help others?

_____
_____
_____
_____

Whatever you wrote above, ask God if this is where you have been placed by Him to work and serve. Write that prayer out to him now.

A Man Loves His Work

_____
_____
_____
_____

Do you get excited or sad when it's time to go to work? Explain why? Or, why not.

_____
_____
_____
_____

Chapter 6

A Man Walks in Integrity

Proverbs 20:7 (MEV)

**⁷ The just man walks in his integrity;
his children are blessed after him.**

A man knows that his integrity is more precious to him than anything else is. Integrity is the ability to present oneself as truthful, factual, accurate and complete. In other words, a man is always known for his transparency. He is not two faced! He doesn't try to be something that he is not. The person that others see in public is the person that he is in private.

> **The person others see in public is the person that he is in private.**

His reputation is an exact reflection of who is really is. A man knows that he isn't just acting a certain way in front of people just for the moment. He knows that his actions have long-term consequences that will impact his family and legacy. What we do today will have a long lasting effect on our family's name and the way people look at us when doing business or any other activity with us in the future. A man's integrity is closely linked to his name. Whenever we meet others, isn't it interesting that the first thing we want to know is their name. Why is that? Well, first, we want to be able to identify with them on a personal level. Secondly, we want to find out if we know them or someone related to them. Thirdly, the reason we do that is to see if there is a family relationship or if there is a positive or negative relationship attached to their name. A name ties people to their reputation. Someone can do something horrible 20 years earlier and no one remembers it until a name is brought up. Once the name is brought up, immediately we can identify the person with the action, be it good or bad. For example, what do you think about when the names Willie Mays, Hank Aaron, Michael Jordan and Jesse Owens are mentioned? Did you notice how immediately you could back to something that they had done? They were all athletes who were great at their respective sports. Now, let's look at these names, John Wilkes Booth, John Hinckley Jr., Jim Jones, Charles Manson and David Koresh. Did you immediately remember that these people killed others? I am sure you did. That is the power of a person's name. Their names immediately ties into their reputation. When people mention your name, what do they immediately think about you? The power of a man's name has a very powerful effect on people that come into contact with them. Every time, others encounter someone with any of the above-mentioned last names, they will want to know if you are related to them. If their reputation is one of integrity, they will be drawn to you. If anyone is related to any of the above last names of people tied to a negative event that took place earlier in history, it will be difficult for them to earn the trust, friendship or acquaintance with people they come into contact with.

Whatever a man's reputation is, that is how he is viewed by people he comes into contact with. A man's reputation can be good or bad. Integrity is the truthfulness of who you are to yourself and to others, even when no one is watching!

A Man Walks in Integrity

> **Integrity is the truthfulness of who you are to yourself and to others, even when no one is watching!**

Now think about your children. If a man has a negative reputation in his community, his children will carry that mark with them as well. It is important that a man's reputation is known to be one of integrity in all regards, as it will have an effect on his children for generations to come. Therefore, a man will strive to have a positive reputation. He will work at being a man of Godly integrity. As a result, his children will be blessed as well. The scripture says that his *children* are *blessed after him*, when he has laid a foundation of *integrity* that is *just*. How are you known around the town where you live? How are you known where you work? How are you known in your family? How are you known in your house among your wife and kids? The greatest blessing a man can give his children is a good name tied to a great reputation.

> **The greatest blessing a man can give his children is a good name tied to a great reputation.**

How you are known, has an impact on you and your family's future. A man knows that his actions have a long-lasting impact on his family and their future interaction with others.

> **A man knows that his actions have a long-lasting impact on his family and their future interaction with others.**

Reflection

What is integrity?

_____

_____

_____

How do you think other people describe you?

_____

_____

_____

What do you plan to do to make your reputation better regardless of how good or bad it may be now?

_____

_____

_____

A Man Walks in Integrity

Why is a man's integrity so important?

_____

_____

_____

Chapter 7

A Man Possesses Wisdom

Proverbs 12:8 (MEV)
⁸ A man will be <u>commended</u> according to his <u>wisdom</u>, but he who is of a perverse heart will be despised.

A man possesses great wisdom! Never forget that knowledge and wisdom are two different things! Wisdom is more than a person knowing a lot about something. Knowing a lot about something is acquired knowledge. On the other hand, wisdom is different. Wisdom is knowing what and when to do with that *"something"* that has been acquired through knowledge.

A Man Possesses Wisdom

> **Wisdom is knowing what and when to do with that *"something"* that has been acquired through knowledge.**

A man of wisdom weighs all that he has knowledge of before he acts in haste. He will always be cautious and mindful of all that he has been exposed to in gathering any type of information to be used in his life. He knows that patience and wisdom go hand in hand concerning situations he is faced with in his life. A man is cautious when faced with decisions that must be made every day. He always thinks about the long-term impact of his decisions. He knows his decisions are eternal and once they are made, tremendous effort must be put forth to lessen any ill-formed decision he might make. Therefore, a man is not afraid to seek advice from other Godly men when he has to make decisions. As Proverbs 15:22 says, [22] *Without counsel, purposes are*

A Man Possesses Wisdom

disappointed, but in the multitude of counselors they are established. In other words, a man knows that in order to reduce the chance of failing when faced with a decision that has to be made, he needs to find like-minded Godly men to pray and advise him in the best path that God is leading him towards. Simply stated, a man doesn't let his ego get in the way of wise counsel that will secure his decision with God's blessing. Egos have destroyed kingdoms, businesses, marriages and relationships. Egos will fool us into thinking we don't need help from anyone to help us with anything.

> **Egos will fool us into thinking we don't need help from anyone to help us with anything.**

Nothing can be further from the truth. When men can come together, touch, and agree with God's will, mountains are moved! Curses

A Man Possesses Wisdom

are broken! Deliverances take place! When men counsel each other, purposes are established, dreams are fulfilled and destinies are placed in motion. In other words, every man needs someone to confide and share his thoughts with concerning his journey in this life. God has placed men in our lives that are waiting to assist us in becoming all He designed us to become. One of the greatest advisers God has placed in our lives on this earth for our success in making decisions is a Pastor. A Pastor is someone that God has placed on this earth to make sure that you stay on the right path of your journey in doing all God wants you to do. Your Pastor will speak into your life without you ever sharing anything about your life to him. If your Senior Pastor is a woman, God will speak through her and there will be a male Pastor in your church that God will move through to guide you in your direction that you need help with. You should never be afraid to seek help and

A Man Possesses Wisdom

guidance. A man relishes having wise friends that God has placed in his life to help him on his journey. A man is wise because he knows where to find wisdom when he can't find it himself.

> **A man is wise because he knows where to find wisdom when he can't find it himself.**

Wisdom always leads a man to another man when he needs help. Wisdom advises a man when he needs advice. Wisdom can only establish a man when he chooses to follow its path! If it costs everything, a man is not afraid to obtain wisdom.

A Man Possesses Wisdom

Reflection

What is wisdom?

_____

_____

_____

Why is wisdom important to a man?

_____

_____

_____

Do you have someone that you seek advice from when you are trying to make decisions?

_____

_____

_____

Do you belong to a men's ministry in your church? Why or why not?

A Man Possesses Wisdom

Chapter 8

Only God Can Make a Man

Genesis 2:7 (MEV)

> **⁷ Then <u>the LORD God formed man</u> from the dust of the ground and breathed into his nostrils the breath of life, and man became a living being.**

Make no mistake about it. Only God can make a man. To make a man requires that God shape, fashion, frame and form him. A woman can't make a man. Only God can do that. She can only give birth to a man.

> **A woman can't make a man. Only God can do that. She can only give birth to a man.**

In fact, until God makes the man, he is not ready to unite with a woman. Only after God shapes, forms, fashions and frames a man, is he able to unite with a woman. God's original design was for a man to make a woman, not for a woman to make a man.

> **God's original design was for a man to make a woman, not for a woman to make a man.**

Ever notice how women are drawn to singers, movie stars, athletes and successful executives? She is drawn to them because when she sees them, she sees how God designed for her to be cared and provided for. How much more is she attracted to a man that has been made by God. She is drawn to his godliness, security, love, prosperity, holiness, strength, purpose, vision and courage. When a woman sees these qualities in a man, she can't help but respond in the way God designed her to respond, which is to be in a state of awe, reverence, peace, security and completeness. Always remember that a woman is the outward expression of an inward man that has been shaped by God. Take a moment and think about that.

> **A woman is the outward expression of an inward man that has been shaped by God.**

Genesis 2:22 shows us, *²² Then <u>the rib</u> which the LORD God had <u>taken from man</u>, He <u>made into a woman</u>, and He brought her to the man.* Notice that she was brought to the man only after being made by the man, whom first had to be made by God. A woman will always be attracted to the God she sees in the man from where she came from first before she is attracted to anything else about him.

> **A woman will always be attracted to the God she sees in the man from where she came from first before she is attracted to anything else about him.**

In other words, she will be attracted to his God like characteristics such as his strength, authority, wisdom, boldness, vision, stature and style. Sadly, most will see these characteristics in those whom have been successful by the world's standards versus God's holiness. Also note that, when a man has been made, fashioned and shaped with divine godlike characteristics, he will not have to look for his wife; his wife will be brought to him by God himself. Genesis 2:22 shows us, [22] *...and He brought her to the man.*

> **When a man has been made, fashioned and shaped with divine godlike characteristics, he will not have to look for his wife; his wife will be brought to him by God himself.**

Isn't it exciting to know that we don't have to try to impress a woman on our own merit? All we have to do is walk in godlike character and our mate will be special delivered to us by God himself.

There is more to this. Not only is a woman attracted and brought to a man made by God, the man will get excited when he sees whom God designed especially for him to walk through life's journey with. She will become the apple of his eye, the most beautiful sight he has ever laid his eyes on. He will love her mightily because when he sees her, he sees himself. He should see himself, when he sees the woman God made for him, because she is the outward expression of his inward self!

> **She will become the apple of his eye, the most beautiful sight he has ever laid his eyes on. He will love her mightily because when he sees her, he sees himself.**

We see in Ephesians 5:28 where it says, ²⁸ In this way *men ought to love their wives* as their *own bodies.* He who loves his wife loves himself. ²⁹ For no one ever *hated his own flesh*, but *nourishes* and *cherishes* it, just as the Lord cares for the church. Also, Genesis 2:23 says, *²³ Then Adam said, "This is now bone of my bones and flesh of my flesh; she will be called Woman, for she was taken out of Man.*

When a woman lets God make a man first, he can't help but love her when he sees her. His love will be expressed by the *nurturing* and *cherishing* that she will receive. He will not physically, mentally or emotionally abuse her or be bitter towards her at all. He is a man that has been made by God to love the one that God brings to him because he will see himself in her. He will make her, strengthen her, encourage her, support her and honor her. This is how he will show his love through nurturing and cherishing her. A man made by God will take a woman where she never even dreamed about or thought she would ever go. He will teach her how to pray as she never prayed before. He will teach her about scripture and the Bible and show her things she never saw before in the word of God. He will teach her how to dream like she never dreamed before. He will teach her how to have things she never thought she could ever have before. He will simply make her into everything God intended for her to become. He will make her into the woman that God designed her to be.

Only God Can Make a Man

This is why the two will become one flesh. When a man and woman unite, they become one flesh. God gives them the same identical Spirit to operate in the power of one person in the earthly realm in unity. They are accomplishing His will and purpose for their lives by displaying unity in all that they do in their fleshly state while here on earth. In other words, they will think, plan and move together. They will pursue and accomplish everything that God ever desired and willed for them to have. Most people don't know that when a man and woman become husband and wife, they become closer than the father, mother and child relationship that exists in a typical family unit. They become closer than a typical family because when they marry, they literally share the same blood when they consummate the marriage and become one person in the eyes of God. That is why the Bible says that they become one flesh. Additionally, they are now in a relationship with

God to fulfill His kingdom purpose for their lives through Him.

We see in Genesis 2:24 where it says, [24] Therefore *a man* will *leave his father* and his *mother* and be *joined* to *his wife*, and *they will become one flesh*. This is a mystery to some but should be a common understanding to those that are saved by Christ! This scripture means that, the original relationship and family was designed as husband and wife, not father, mother and child, but husband and wife. Why? Because when a man and woman marry, they become one in unity and operate as one. They are a unit now, operating together in harmony. Another way to look at it is this way; they now function as one and not as separated pieces. That's right! We literally operate together to accomplish something in the same spirit, emotion, strategy etc. when we become united in marriage. When we become married, our thoughts are no longer split in different directions. We have a mate that will share our same thoughts. When it is something that we want to do or accomplish, we will not go about it alone on a separate journey. We will have a suitable mate that will be with us on the journey to accomplish all God called us to do. All of God's blessings are released in our lives. A man is a fragment of himself until he unites with the wholeness of his wife.

> **A man is a fragment of himself until he unites with the wholeness of his wife.**

Man was not designed to go through life alone. He was designed to have a suitable helper. His wife helps him complete God's design for their lives and he helps her do the same. It is reciprocal. Have you been made by God? Only you can answer that question.

Only God Can Make a Man

Remember that a man can only be made by God. God will do that directly and through other men of God. Pray to God and ask Him to begin to make you into a man of God. Ask Him to send men of God in your life that you can have as living examples to follow. Get involved in a local church and join the men's ministry. Find a mentor that is a Christian and ask him to walk with you on your journey to manhood. Manhood is a great responsibility and you will need all the right training to become all God designed you to be on this earth.

Reflection

What does it mean to be made by God?

_____

_____

_____

Can a woman make a man?

_____

_____

_____

Was God's original design for a man to make a woman? Explain your answer.

_____

_____

_____

_____

Epilogue

The best way to become a man is for you to give your life to Christ Jesus. Repeat these simple words and it will be a done deal. Repeat the following: Lord Christ Jesus as of this very moment, I accept you as Lord and Savior of my life. I now give my life to you to be fashioned for your purpose and glory. Lord, all of these things that I have said, I truly believe in my heart and have confessed with my mouth to you. I know now that I have received everlasting life based on the work that Christ has done and will continue to do in my life. Lord Christ, thank you for bringing me to this point of my life where I surrender my all to you. It is in the Holy Spirit through Christ Jesus, I say Amen.

Humbly Yours in Christ

Apostle Jamie T. Pleasant

Epilogue

Books by Dr. Pleasant

Book Dr. Pleasant for a Speaking Engagement

For speaking engagements, please contact Dr. Jamie T. Pleasant at admin@newzionchristianchurch.org or 678.845.7055

Books by Dr. Pleasant

These books can be purchased at any bookstore or online at amazon.com, barnesandnoble.com and many other stores and outlets.

About the Author

Apostle Jamie T. Pleasant; Ph.D. is the Chief Executive Pastor and Founder of New Zion Christian Church in Suwanee, Georgia. As a modern day polymath, he holds a bachelor's degree in Physics from Benedict College in Columbia, South Carolina, Marketing Studies from Clemson University and an M.B.A. in Marketing from Clark Atlanta University. On August 13, 1999, Apostle Pleasant achieved a Georgia Tech milestone by becoming the first African American to graduate with a Ph.D. in Business Management in the school's 111 plus year history.

God gave him the vision to establish a Biblically based economic development initiative for New Zion Christian Church. He remains at the pulse of the economic business sector. As a result,

Apostle Pleasant is in constant demand to train, speak and teach others at all levels in ministries and the private sector about business and economic development across the country. He has created cutting edge and industry leading ministerial programs in the church such as The Financial Literacy Academy for Youth (FLAFY), where youth from the ages of 13-19 attend 12 week intense classes on financial money management principles. At the end of 12 weeks, they receive a "Personal Finance" certificate of achievement. Other ministries he has pioneered include; The Wealth Builders Investment Club (WBIC), which educates and allows members to actively invest in the stock market, along with the much celebrated Institute of Entrepreneurship (IOE), where participants earn a certificate in Entrepreneurship after three months of comprehensive training in all aspects of starting and owning a successful competitive business.

The main goal and purpose of the IOE is that each year one of the trained students will be awarded up to $10,000 start up money to ensure financial success. The newly added SAT & PSAT prep courses for children ages 9-19 fuels the potential success of all who walk through the doors of New Zion Christian Church.

Apostle Pleasant has met with political officials such as President Clinton and Nelson Mandela. He has delivered the opening prayer for the born again Christian and comedian, Steve Harvey. He has performed marriage ceremonies and counseled numerous celebrated personalities such as Usher Raymond (Confessions Recording Artist), Terri Vaughn (Lavita Jenkins on The Steve Harvey Show), and many others.

He is civically engaged as well. After the Columbine High School shooting, he founded the National School Safety Advocacy Association. His latest foundations include the Young

Entrepreneurship Program (YEP) and the African American Consumer Economic Rights Inc (AACER).

He has authored ten (10) books, *Prayers That Open Heaven, Capturing and Keeping the Pastor's Heart, Powerful Prayers That Open Heaven, Advertising Principles: How to Effectively Reach African Americans in the 21st Century, Discover a New You: A 21 Day Journey to Uncovering Your Uniqueness, From My Heart To Yours: Love Letters From A Loving Father, Today's Apostle: Servants of God, Leading His People towards Unity , Strategic Health Marketing: Marketing Mix and Segmentation Strategies, Daily Quotes for Daily Blessings* and *The Making of a Man* .

Dr. Pleasant is the husband of Kimberly Pleasant (whom he loves dearly) and the proud father of three children: Christian, Zion and Nacara.

FINI

www.ingramcontent.com/pod-product-compliance
Lightning Source LLC
Chambersburg PA
CBHW021020090426
42738CB00007B/848